IT'S A
LONG WAY TO
TIPPERARY

PEANUTS CLASSICS

Dr. Beagle and Mr. Hyde
Fly, You Stupid Kite, Fly!
How Long, Great Pumpkin, How Long?
It's Great to Be a Superstar
Kiss Her, You Blockhead!
My Anxieties Have Anxieties
Speak Softly, and Carry a Beagle
There Goes the Shutout
Summers Fly, Winters Walk
Thank Goodness for People
The Beagle Has Landed
What Makes You Think You're Happy?
And a Woodstock in a Birch Tree
A Smile Makes a Lousy Umbrella
The Mad Punter Strikes Again
There's a Vulture Outside
Here Comes the April Fool!
What Makes Musicians So Sarcastic?
A Kiss on the Nose Turns Anger Aside
It's Hard Work Being Bitter
I'm Not Your Sweet Babboo!
Stop Snowing on My Secretary
Always Stick Up for the Underbird
What's Wrong with Being Crabby?
Don't Hassle Me with Your Sighs, Chuck
The Way of the Fussbudget Is Not Easy
You're Weird, Sir!
It's a Long Way to Tipperary

IT'S A LONG WAY TO TIPPERARY

Copr. © 1952, 1958 United Feature Syndicate, Inc.

by Charles M. Schulz

An Owl Book
Henry Holt and Company/ New York

Henry Holt and Company, Inc.
Publishers since 1866
115 West 18th Street
New York, New York 10011

Henry Holt® is a registered trademark
of Henry Holt and Company, Inc.

Library of Congress Catalog Card Number:
93-77678

ISBN 0-8050-2696-7 (An Owl Book: pbk.)

New Owl Book Edition—1993

Originally published by
Holt, Rinehart and Winston in 1967
as *You'll Flip, Charlie Brown*. Published in an
expanded edition under the title *It's a
Long Way to Tipperary* in 1976 and included
strips from *The Unsinkable Charlie Brown*,
published in 1966 by Holt, Rinehart and Winston.

Printed in the United States of America
All first editions are printed on acid-free paper.∞

1 3 5 7 9 10 8 6 4 2

HELLO, KITE-EATING TREE!

IT LOOKS LIKE YOU'VE PUT ON A LITTLE WEIGHT SINCE I LAST SAW YOU... YOU LOOK A LITTLE TALLER, TOO

BUT YOU HAVEN'T HAD ANY KITES LATELY, HAVE YOU?

WELL, YOU'RE NOT GOING TO GET THIS KITE, YOU DIRTY KITE-EATING TREE! I'LL FLY IT CLEAR OVER ON THE OTHER SIDE OF TOWN JUST TO SPITE YOU! YOU CAN STARVE, DO YOU HEAR?!

YOU'RE PRACTICALLY DROOLING, AREN'T YOU? YOU HAVEN'T EATEN A KITE FOR MONTHS, AND YOU'RE JUST DYING TO GET HOLD OF THIS ONE, AREN'T YOU? AREN'T YOU?

WELL, YOU'RE NOT, DO YOU HEAR ME? YOU'RE NOT!

HERE.. TAKE IT

IT'S BEEN A LONG WINTER, AND I'M VERY TENDER-HEARTED..

CHOMP! CHOMP! CHOMP!

YOU HATE THAT TREE, DON'T YOU CHARLIE BROWN?

IT'S A KITE-EATING TREE, AND I HATE IT!

YOU KNOW WHY I HATE IT? BECAUSE IT'S GREEDY, THAT'S WHY! EVEN WHILE IT HAS A KITE IN ITS BRANCHES, IT'LL REACH OUT AND GRAB ANOTHER ONE! IT'S LIKE A LITTLE KID EATING FRENCH FRIES

YOU DIRTY KITE-EATING TREE!

WHEN CHARLIE BROWN HATES SOMETHING, HE REALLY HATES IT!

IN KITE-FLYING, THE RATIO OF WEIGHT TO SAIL-AREA IS VERY IMPORTANT

THIS RATIO IS KNOWN AS "SAIL LOADING" AND IT IS MEASURED IN OUNCES PER SQUARE FOOT..FOR EXAMPLE, A THREE-FOOT FLAT KITE WITH A SAIL AREA OF FOUR AND ONE-HALF SQUARE FEET SHOULD WEIGH ABOUT TWO OR THREE OUNCES...

YOU KNOW A LOT ABOUT KITES, DON'T YOU, CHARLIE BROWN?

YES I THINK I CAN SAY THAT I DO...

THEN WHY IS YOUR KITE DOWN THE SEWER?

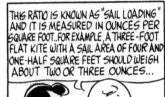

HOW CAN YOU TELL A "KITE-EATING" TREE FROM AN ORDINARY TREE?

YOU CAN'T UNTIL YOU SEE A KITE CAUGHT BY ONE... AN ORDINARY TREE WILL LET A KITE GO RIGHT AWAY, BUT A KITE-EATING TREE WILL HANG ON TO A KITE FOR WEEKS!

THEY CLUTCH KITES IN THEIR GREEDY BRANCHES, AND SLOWLY DEVOUR THEM! IT'S A SHOCKING SIGHT... THEY EAT THE PAPER LIKE IT WAS FRIED CHICKEN, AND SPIT OUT THE STICKS LIKE BONES!

ANY ONE OF THESE TREES COULD BE A MONSTROUS KITE-EATING TREE... YOU JUST CAN'T TELL...

BRRR!

MY KITE IS UP! IT'S UP! IT'S UP!

NO, IT'S GOING DOWN! STAY UP, YOU FOOL!

DON'T GET NEAR THAT KITE-EATING TREE!

LOOK OUT! LOOK OUT!

OH, NO! OH, GOOD GRIEF! OH, NO! OH, NO!

OH, NO!

AAUGH!

THAT'S THE MOST GRUESOME THING I'VE EVER SEEN....

SCHULZ

THE STRANGEST THING JUST HAPPENED...
I WAS STANDING OUT ON THE LAWN
WHEN ALL OF A SUDDEN THIS BIG PILE
OF STRING WALKED BY!

I THINK YOU AND THAT
BLANKET NEED A LONG REST

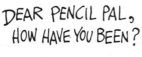

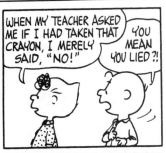

GOOD NIGHT, OL' PAL... SEE YOU IN THE MORNING...

I'M HUNGRY!

ARE YOU OUT OF YOUR MIND? GO BACK TO SLEEP!

MY HEAD MAY GO TO SLEEP, BUT MY STOMACH WILL BE AWAKE ALL NIGHT!

ALL RIGHT, WAKE UP! YOU'RE THE ONE WHO WAS SO HUNGRY LAST NIGHT... HERE'S YOUR BREAKFAST!

RATS! NOW, MY HEAD'S AWAKE, BUT MY STOMACH'S ASLEEP!

SCHULZ

I FEEL GUILTY ABOUT THE WAY I FEED SNOOPY...HIS MEALS ARE SO DRAB...

I SHOULD DO SOMETHING TO MAKE HIS MEALS MORE INTERESTING..

WELL, SNOOPY, WHAT ARE YOUR PLANS FOR TODAY?

PLANS? I HADN'T EVEN THOUGHT ABOUT IT...

BUT I SUPPOSE I'LL SLEEP A LITTLE THIS MORNING...THEN, THIS AFTERNOON, I'LL TAKE A SHORT NAP, AND LATER ON I'LL TRY TO GET SOME MORE SLEEP...

THOSE ARE GOOD PLANS

SUPPERTIME!

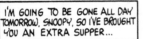

I'M GOING TO BE GONE ALL DAY TOMORROW, SNOOPY, SO I'VE BROUGHT YOU AN EXTRA SUPPER...

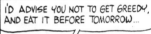

I'D ADVISE YOU NOT TO GET GREEDY, AND EAT IT BEFORE TOMORROW...

AAUGH!

I'M GLAD I ATE IT... I WOULD HAVE HATED MYSELF IF TOMORROW NEVER CAME!

HMM..

LET'S SEE..WE'LL HAVE TO HAVE A STATION WAGON, A TOWN CAR AND A SPORTS CAR...OUR HOME SHOULD BE IN AT LEAST THE ONE-HUNDRED-THOUSAND CLASS... DO PIANO PLAYERS MAKE A LOT OF MONEY?

I DON'T KNOW...I SUPPOSE IT DEPENDS ON HOW HARD THEY PRACTICE...

I SEE..

WELL, I'LL PROBABLY NEED A HALF DOZEN FUR COATS, AT LEAST THIRTY SKI OUTFITS AND ABOUT FIFTY FORMALS...I'LL NEEDS LOTS OF JEWELRY AND EXOTIC PERFUMES AND I'LL NEED ABOUT A HUNDRED PAIRS OF SHOES...

WE'LL HAVE TO HAVE A SWIMMING POOL, OLYMPIC SIZE, HEATED, AND RIDING HORSES, A TENNIS COURT AND A HUGE FORMAL GARDEN...WE WILL TRAVEL EXTENSIVELY, OF COURSE; ROUND-THE-WORLD CRUISES...THAT SORT OF THING...AND...

KEEP PRACTICING, KID!

I CAN'T SLEEP!

MAYBE IF I MOVE AROUND AND TRY DIFFERENT POSITIONS...

RATS! I JUST CAN'T GET COMFORTABLE!

SNOOPY?

SNOOPY?

WHERE'D HE GO?

Z

HERE...I BROUGHT YOU A PIECE OF TOAST

WELL, THANK YOU

"THANK YOU, DEAR SISTER"

THANK YOU, DEAR SISTER

"THANK YOU, DEAR SISTER..GREATEST OF ALL SISTERS"

THANK YOU, DEAR SISTER..GREATEST OF ALL SISTERS!

"THANK YOU, DEAR SISTER, GREATEST OF ALL SISTERS, WITHOUT WHOM I'D NEVER SURVIVE!"

THANK YOU, DEAR SISTER, GREATEST OF ALL SISTERS, WITHOUT WHOM I'D NEVER SURVIVE!

YOU'RE VERY WELCOME

HOW CAN I EAT WHEN I FEEL NAUSEATED?

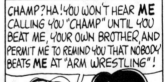

THIS IS WHAT I ENJOY.. A MID-AFTERNOON SNACK...

I THINK I LIKE CEREAL MORE IN THE AFTERNOON THAN I DO IN THE MORNING...

NOW, I HAVE TO FIND SOMETHING TO READ WHILE I EAT MY COLD CEREAL, AND I HAVE TO FIND IT FAST BEFORE THE CEREAL GETS SOGGY...

I CAN'T STAND TO EAT COLD CEREAL WITHOUT HAVING SOMETHING TO READ..

RATS! SOMEBODY TOOK THE SPORTS SECTION OUT OF THE MORNING PAPER! AND WHERE'S THE FUNNIES? THEY TOOK THE FUNNIES, TOO! GOOD GRIEF!

"MOBY DICK"...NO, I DON'T WANT TO START THAT RIGHT NOW..."THE INTERPRETER'S BIBLE"...TWELVE VOLUMES...THAT'S A LITTLE TOO MUCH FOR ONE BOWL OF CEREAL.."BLEAK HOUSE"...NO.."JOSEPH ANDREWS"...NO..

THIS IS TERRIBLE! I'VE GOT TO FIND SOMETHING FAST!

COMIC MAGAZINES! HAVE I READ ALL OF THEM?

I'VE READ THAT ONE, AND THAT ONE, AND THIS ONE, AND THAT ONE, AND THIS ONE, AND THIS ONE, AND...

I HAVEN'T READ THIS ONE!

SOGGY!

SCHULZ

PSYCHIAT HELP 5¢

SIT DOWN, PLEASE

THANK YOU

THE DOCTOR IS IN

PSYCHIATRIC HELP 5¢

I'M GOING TO ASK YOU A QUESTION, AND I WANT YOU TO ANSWER ME TRUTHFULLY

THE DOCTOR IS IN

YOU SEE, PHYSICIANS CAN LEARN A LOT ABOUT A PATIENT BY ASKING WHAT MAY EVEN SOUND LIKE A VERY SIMPLE QUESTION..

ALL RIGHT, NOW ANSWER ME TRUTHFULLY... WHICH DO YOU PREFER, A SUNRISE OR A SUNSET?

WELL, A SUNSET, I GUESS..

THE DOCTOR IS IN

I THOUGHT SO! YOU'RE JUST THE TYPE! I MIGHT HAVE KNOWN! WHAT A DISAPPOINTMENT!

THE DOCTOR IS IN

PEOPLE WHO PREFER SUNSETS ARE DREAMERS! THEY ALWAYS GIVE UP! THEY ALWAYS LOOK BACK INSTEAD OF FORWARD! I JUST MIGHT HAVE KNOWN YOU WEREN'T A SUNRISE PERSON!

SUNRISERS ARE GO-GETTERS! THEY HAVE AMBITION AND DRIVE! GIVE ME A PERSON WHO LIKES A SUNRISE EVERY TIME! YES, SIR!

THE DOCTOR IS IN

I'M SORRY, CHARLIE BROWN... IF YOU PREFER SUNSETS TO SUNRISES, I CAN'T TAKE YOUR CASE... YOU'RE HOPELESS!

THE DOCTOR IS IN

ACTUALLY, I'VE ALWAYS SORT OF PREFERRED NOON!

THE DOCTOR IS IN

SCHULZ

HAPPY BEETHOVEN'S BIRTHDAY!

ON BEETHOVEN'S BIRTHDAY IT IS CUSTOMARY TO KISS SOMEONE YOU LIKE RIGHT SQUACK ON THE NOSE

SQUACK!

THAT COULD START A STAMPEDE TO BRAHMS!

WHEN JULIET ASKS,"O ROMEO, ROMEO, WHEREFORE ART THOU ROMEO?" SHE IS NOT WONDERING WHERE HE IS...

RATHER, SHE IS COMMENTING ON THE FACT OF HIS BEING NAMED ROMEO!

NOW THAT I KNOW THAT, WHAT DO I DO?

I WORRY ABOUT THIS TIME OF YEAR..

I REMEMBER LAST YEAR ABOUT THIS TIME...IT WAS TWO O'CLOCK IN THE MORNING, AND I WAS SOUND ASLEEP...

SUDDENLY, OUT OF NOWHERE, THIS CRAZY GUY WITH A SLED LANDS RIGHT ON MY ROOF

HE WAS OKAY, BUT THOSE STUPID REINDEER KEPT STEPPING ON MY STOMACH!

RATS!

I DON'T UNDERSTAND IT...

HOW COME SOME PEOPLE GET NO CHRISTMAS CARDS WHILE OTHER PEOPLE GET A WHOLE LOT OF THEM?

SOME OF US HAVE MORE FRIENDS

GRAMMA SAYS WHEN SHE WAS LITTLE, SHE USED TO HANG UP HER STOCKING ON CHRISTMAS EVE...

THEN, WHEN CHRISTMAS MORNING CAME, SHE'D RUN DOWNSTAIRS, AND FIND IT FILLED WITH APPLES AND ORANGES...

I CAN SEE IT NOW... THREE GRAPES!

Dear Santa Claus,

Just a last note before you take off.

I hope you have a nice trip.

Don't forget to fasten your seat belt.

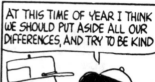

DECEMBER 25

DEAR GRAMPA AND GRANDMA,

WHAT ARE YOU DOING?

THANK YOU FOR THE CHRISTMAS PRESENT.

ARE YOU TRYING TO MAKE ME LOOK BAD?

I WAS REAL HAPPY TO GET THE DOLLAR.

YOU'RE WRITING A "THANK YOU" NOTE RIGHT AWAY JUST TO MAKE ME LOOK BAD, AREN'T YOU?

IT WAS VERY THOUGHTFUL OF YOU.

YOUR KIND DRIVE ME CRAZY! WHY DO YOU HAVE TO BE SO EFFICIENT?! WHY DO YOU HAVE TO...

LUCY ENJOYED HER GIFT, TOO, AND SAYS TO THANK YOU VERY VERY MUCH.

!

LOVE, Linus

IF YOU'LL WAIT A MINUTE, I'LL RUN AND GET YOU AN AIR MAIL STAMP!

ARE YOU GOING TO BE A NEWSPAPER BOY WHEN YOU GET OLDER, CHARLIE BROWN?

WELL, I'D LIKE TO BE... YES, I THINK I'D LIKE TO HAVE MY OWN ROUTE..

THEN YOU SHOULD LEARN HOW TO ROLL AND FOLD A PAPER SO YOU CAN TOSS IT ONTO A DOOR STEP...HERE, LET ME SHOW YOU...

SEE, YOU FOLD IT ACROSS THE SECOND COLUMN LIKE THIS...THEN YOU ROLL IT LIKE THIS UNTIL YOU GET IT LIKE THIS, AND THEN YOU TUCK THIS PART IN HERE, AND TWIST IT LIKE THIS...

NOW YOU'RE ALL SET TO...

THROW IT!

ANOTHER THING YOU HAVE TO BE ABLE TO DO IS GET CUSTOMERS. IF YOU WANT TO KNOW ABOUT THAT, FEEL FREE TO ASK..

THANK YOU..

THAT'S YOUR PINK WOOL SKIRT...THESE ARE THE TWO SWEATERS I HAD IN THERE...

THANK YOU, SNOOPY..

YOU'RE WELCOME

EVERYONE IN THE NEIGHBORHOOD USES MY CEDAR CLOSET!

SCHULZ

IT'S FAIR WEATHER TODAY, CHARLIE BROWN..

SO WHERE ARE ALL MY FRIENDS?

SCHULZ

WHY DO THINGS LIKE THIS ALWAYS HAPPEN TO ME?

BECAUSE I DON'T DO MY HOMEWORK, THAT'S WHY THINGS LIKE THIS ALWAYS HAPPEN TO ME!

I'M DOOMED! IF THAT BELL DOESN'T RING PRETTY SOON, I'M DOOMED!

I SHOULD HAVE DONE THAT REPORT, AND THEN I WOULDN'T HAVE HAD TO WORRY LIKE THIS...

OH, PLEASE DON'T CALL ON ME...PLEASE, DON'T!

WHY DOESN'T THAT STUPID BELL RING? COME ON, BELL....RING! TAKE ME OFF THE HOOK!

PLEASE DON'T CALL ON ME TODAY... WAIT UNTIL TOMORROW...PLEASE DON'T CALL ON ME....PLEASE! PLEASE! PLEASE! PLEASE!

COME ON, YOU STUPID BELL, RING! DON'T JUST HANG THERE ON THE WALL! RING! COME ON! RING!!

OH, I'M DOOMED! SHE'S GOING TO CALL ON ME NEXT, AND I'M NOT READY, AND..

RRRING!!

OH, MAN, WHAT A CLOSE CALL! I THOUGHT FOR SURE SHE WAS GOING TO CALL ON ME...I THOUGHT I WAS DOOMED!

NOW, YOU CAN GO HOME AND FINISH YOUR REPORT, HUH, CHARLIE BROWN? THEN YOU WON'T HAVE TO WORRY ABOUT IT TOMORROW...

WHO CARES ABOUT TOMORROW? C'MON, LET'S PLAY BALL!

DID YOU SEE THE BULLETIN BOARD? GOOD LUCK, CHARLIE BROWN!

"THE FOLLOWING STUDENTS WILL BE PARTNERS IN THIS SEMESTER'S SCIENCE PROJECTS..STUDENTS WHO DO NOT DO A PROJECT WILL RECEIVE A FAILING GRADE."

GOOD GRIEF! I'VE BEEN PAIRED WITH THAT PRETTY, LITTLE RED-HAIRED GIRL! HOW CAN I BE HER PARTNER? I CAN'T EVEN **TALK** TO HER!

SUDDENLY I HAVE THE FEELING OF IMPENDING DOOM!

OH, OH! THAT LITTLE RED-HAIRED GIRL IS LOOKING AT THE BULLETIN BOARD..

NOW SHE KNOWS THAT THE TEACHER HAS MADE US PARTNERS IN THE SCIENCE PROJECT! MAYBE SHE'LL COME OVER HERE AND SAY, "HI, CHARLIE BROWN..I SEE YOU AND I ARE PARTNERS!"

MAYBE SHE'LL EVEN OFFER TO SHAKE HANDS...I'LL BET HER HANDS ARE SMOOTH AND COOL...

MY HEAD IS HOT AND STUPID!

SCHULZ

I SAW THE BULLETIN BOARD, CHARLIE BROWN..

YOU AND THAT LITTLE RED-HAIRED GIRL ARE SUPPOSED TO BE PARTNERS IN A SCIENCE PROJECT...ANYONE NOT DOING A SCIENCE PROJECT WILL GET A FAILING GRADE..THAT'S WHAT IT SAID!

WELL, I GUESS THAT MEANS I JUST HAVE TO GO OVER AND INTRODUCE MYSELF TO HER...I'LL GO OVER AND SAY,"HI, PARTNER"... I'LL... I'LL.....

I'LL TAKE THE FAILING GRADE!

YOU'RE BEING RIDICULOUS, CHARLIE BROWN

I CAN'T HELP IT..

I CAN'T JUST GO UP TO THAT LITTLE RED-HAIRED GIRL AND TALK TO HER.. SHE HAS A PRETTY FACE, AND PRETTY FACES MAKE ME NERVOUS...

HOW COME MY FACE DOESN'T MAKE YOU NERVOUS? HUH?!

I NOTICE YOU CAN TALK TO ME! I HAVE A PRETTY FACE! HOW COME YOU CAN TALK TO ME?!

TO THE OFFICE? YES, MA'AM..

I'VE BEEN CALLED TO THE OFFICE! WHY SHOULD I BE CALLED TO THE OFFICE? I HAVEN'T DONE ANYTHING WRONG! IT CAN'T BE ABOUT OUR SCIENCE PROJECT..THAT ISN'T DUE FOR A WEEK

MAYBE SOMETHING HAPPENED AT HOME! MAYBE SOMEONE IS SICK...I USUALLY NEVER GET CALLED TO THE OFFICE... WHY SHOULD THEY CALL ME? WHY ME? I HAVEN'T DONE ANYTHING...

OFFICE WHY DO YOU PERSECUTE ME?

CHARLIE BROWN GOT SENT TO THE OFFICE..

HE DIDN'T GET "SENT".... HE WAS CALLED! THERE'S A BIG DIFFERENCE, YOU KNOW!

SHH! LOOK, HE'S COMING BACK.. CHARLIE BROWN IS COMING BACK FROM THE PRINCIPAL'S OFFICE...

MERCY! ? WELL, I'LL BE!!

AHEM!

WELL, WILL YOU LOOK AT THAT? CHARLIE BROWN HAS BEEN PUT ON SAFETY PATROL! HOW ABOUT THAT?

OH, BOY! EVERYONE IS LOOKING AT ME! IF THIS DOESN'T IMPRESS THAT LITTLE RED-HAIRED GIRL, NOTHING WILL!

WHEN I GOT CALLED TO THE OFFICE, I WAS A NOBODY...NOW, I'M A MAN WITH A BADGE!

OKAY, LET'S MOVE ALONG THERE!

JUST PAY ATTENTION TO YOUR SAFETY PATROL! MOVE ALONG, NOW! MOVE ALONG!

"FUZZ"!

OKAY... LET'S MOVE ALONG.... LET'S MOVE ALONG ...LET'S........

I THOUGHT YOU AND THAT LITTLE RED-HAIRED GIRL WERE SUPPOSED TO DO A SCIENCE PROJECT TOGETHER?

WE ARE...DON'T RUSH ME...I HAVE TO TALK TO HER ABOUT IT FIRST...I FIGURE NOW THAT I'M ON SAFETY PATROL SHE'LL BE REAL ANXIOUS TO MEET ME

IF YOU DON'T DO THAT SCIENCE PROJECT, CHARLIE BROWN, YOU'LL GET A FAILING GRADE...AND IF YOU GET A FAILING GRADE, THEY'LL TAKE YOU OFF THE SCHOOL SAFETY PATROL!

THANK YOU, VOICE OF DOOM!

ACTUALLY, THE KINDERGARTEN TEACHER SAYS HE'S ONE OF HER BEST PUPILS!

THE LAST I REMEMBER I WAS STANDING THERE IN THE RAIN HOLDING MY "STOP" SIGN..

WELL, THEY SAY THE CAR ONLY BUMPED YOU, CHARLIE BROWN, BUT IT WAS A VERY CLOSE CALL...

ACTUALLY, I FEEL FINE..I DON'T HAVE A SINGLE PAIN..

I ASKED THAT LITTLE RED-HAIRED GIRL IF SHE WANTED ME TO GIVE YOU ANY MESSAGE...

SHE SAID SHE DIDN'T EVEN REMEMBER WHAT YOU LOOK LIKE!

I HURT ALL OVER!

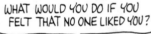

PERHAPS YOU CAN GIVE ME AN ANSWER, LINUS..

WHAT WOULD YOU DO IF YOU FELT THAT NO ONE LIKED YOU?

I'D TRY TO LOOK AT MYSELF OBJECTIVELY, AND SEE WHAT I COULD DO TO IMPROVE...THAT'S MY ANSWER, CHARLIE BROWN

I HATE THAT ANSWER!

SCHULZ

ALL RIGHT! EVERYBODY OUT FOR A LITTLE INFIELD PRACTICE!

I'LL HIT THE BALL TO THIRD BASE..YOU THROW IT TO FIRST...FIRST THROWS IT HOME, THE CATCHER WHIPS IT BACK TO THIRD AND WE THROW IT AROUND THE HORN! OKAY? LET'S GET IT RIGHT THE FIRST TIME! OKAY, HERE WE GO!!

CLIP

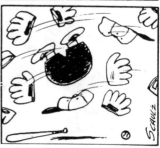

HEY, MANAGER!

AS TEAM SPOKESMAN, I'VE BEEN REQUESTED TO ASK YOU FOR MORE TIME OFF

WHAT SORT OF TIME OFF WOULD YOU LIKE?

WE'D PREFER NOT TO SHOW UP FOR THE GAMES!

YOU'RE NOT A GOOD MANAGER.. YOU KNOW WHY?

YOU SHOULD BE OUT THERE ARGUING WITH THE UMPIRE, AND KICKING DIRT ON HIS SHOES

I'VE NEVER SEEN YOU KICK DIRT ON THE UMPIRE'S SHOES... YOU'RE JUST NOT A GOOD MANAGER, CHARLIE BROWN...

I **MUST** BE A GOOD MANAGER..MY STOMACH HURTS!

WHAT'S GOING ON?

CHARLIE BROWN DOESN'T FEEL WELL.. HIS STOMACH HURTS...

IT'S NERVES, CHARLIE BROWN... YOU TAKE THIS GAME TOO SERIOUSLY.. BE LIKE FRIEDA AND ME...WE DON'T CARE IF WE WIN OR LOSE! **LA DE DA!** WHO CARES?

LA DE DA! WIN OR LOSE! WHO CARES?LA DE DA!WE DON'T CARE!WE DON'T CARE!

FOR SOME REASON, THE PAIN HAS SUDDENLY INCREASED...

BONK!

I CAN'T STAND IT!

OKAY, LUCY, WHERE WERE YOU ON THAT FLY BALL? LET'S START PAYING ATTENTION!

BLEAH!

AND HOW ABOUT YOU? YOU WERE OUT OF POSITION ON THAT DOUBLE-PLAY BALL! YOU BETTER LOOK ALIVE!

BLEAH!

AND YOU SURE HAVEN'T BEEN DOING MUCH OF A JOB BEHIND THE PLATE, SCHROEDER! HOW ABOUT SHOWING SOME LIFE BACK THERE, HUH? HOW ABOUT IT?

BLEAH!

MAYBE I WAS TOO HARD ON THEM...AFTER ALL, I HAVEN'T BEEN DOING TOO WELL MYSELF...IN FACT, MY PITCHING HAS BEEN LOUSY!!

BY GOLLY, CHARLIE BROWN, YOU'D BETTER START PITCHING BETTER BALL!! YOU'D BETTER BUCKLE DOWN OUT HERE!

BLEAH!

SCHULZ

CLOMP!

ALL RIGHT, I SAW THAT! BUT I'M GOING TO PRETEND THAT IT NEVER HAPPENED!

I'M NOT GOING TO MOVE! I'M NOT GOING TO CHASE YOU! IF YOU BRING THAT BALL BACK HERE BEFORE I COUNT TO TEN, WE'LL JUST PRETEND THAT NOTHING HAPPENED!

ONE, TWO, THREE, FOUR, FIVE, SIX, SEVEN, EIGHT, NINE...

THANK YOU... THAT WAS A VERY WISE DECISION!

PFFT!

SIGH

YOU'VE BEEN USING MY TOOTHBRUSH!

OH, DON'T BE SILLY! IT'S AN ELECTRIC TOOTHBRUSH, ISN'T IT? WELL, I JUST USED THE HANDLE!

SEE? THE TOOTHBRUSHES ARE INTERCHANGEABLE! WE JUST USE THE SAME HANDLE...

GOOD GRIEF!

BUT WHAT ABOUT THE ELECTRICITY? DO YOU EXPECT ME TO BRUSH MY TEETH WITH THE SAME DIRTY ELECTRICITY?!

MIGHT AS WELL TURN THIS OFF.. THERE'S NO ONE WATCHING IT...

NO ONE WATCHING IT?

WADDYA MEAN, NO ONE? I'M SOMEONE!

YOU COME BACK HERE, AND TURN ON THIS TV! IF ANYONE IS A SOMEONE, I AM!!!

I DEMAND THAT YOU COME BACK HERE! DO YOU HEAR ME? I'M A REAL SOMEONE!!!

I DEMAND THAT YOU COME BACK HERE, AND TURN ON THIS TV!

IT WAS A LOUSY PROGRAM ANYWAY!

MY MOTHER IS ALWAYS COMPLAINING ABOUT HAVING TO MAKE LUNCHES

WHAT'S SO HARD ABOUT IT? THIS MORNING I TOLD HER I'D MAKE MY OWN LUNCH

AND I DID, TOO! SEE? I MADE MY OWN LUNCH..

EIGHT CANDY BARS!

WE HAD A GOOD TIME AT SCHOOL TODAY..

OUR TEACHER TOOK US ON A FIELD TRIP...WE WENT OUT, AND WE SAW THIS GREAT BIG FIELD

IT WAS A REAL FIELD, AND WE SAW IT! WE STOOD RIGHT THERE, AND WE SAW THAT FIELD!

DO YOU THINK YOU'LL BE GOING ON ANY MORE FIELD TRIPS?

I DOUBT IT..WHEN YOU'VE SEEN ONE FIELD, YOU'VE SEEN THEM ALL

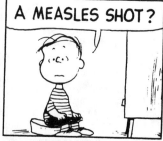

A MEASLES SHOT... GOOD GRIEF!

WHY GET VACCINATED? WHY NOT JUST WEAR SOMETHING RED OR DRINK SOME ELDERBERRY BLOSSOM TEA?

THOSE ARE OLD WIVES' CURES

SOME OF THOSE OLD WIVES WERE PRETTY SHARP!

MY ARM HATES TO GET SHOTS

TELL YOUR ARM NOT TO WORRY... HERE, READ THIS...

"MEASLES IS THE MOST COMMON AND SERIOUS 'CHILDHOOD DISEASE'"...... HMM...

"COMPLICATIONS ARE MIDDLE-EAR INFECTIONS, PNEUMONIA AND EVEN BRAIN DAMAGE"..... WOW!

DID YOU HEAR THAT, ARM? IT'S GOING TO BE WORTH IT!

BLEAH!

WHAT IN THE WORLD **ARE** THOSE?

SOUR MARSHMALLOWS!

OUR FAMILY ATE DINNER AT A RESTAURANT TONIGHT, SNOOPY

I BROUGHT YOU A SUGAR LUMP

THAT SHOULD MAKE ME HAPPY, BUT IT DOESN'T...

IT JUST MAKES ME REALIZE THAT DEEP DOWN HE'D REALLY LIKE TO HAVE A PONY!

SIGH

RE-LIVING PAST GLORIES, CHARLIE BROWN?

YES, I'VE BEEN THINKING ABOUT THE DAY I THREW MY STRIKE!

SNOW!

WHAT A BEAUTIFUL SIGHT...

ALL OF NATURE IS ASLEEP UNDER A BLANKET OF SNOW!

THAT'S TRUE!

TODAY THE NEIGHBORHOOD, TOMORROW THE WORLD!

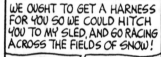

SNOW, SNOW, SNOW!

I WISH IT WAS SUMMER...

I MISS THE BASEBALL SEASON...

I MISS STANDING OUT HERE ON THE PITCHER'S MOUND WITH THE EXCITEMENT OF THE GAME ALL AROUND ME...

LADIES AND GENTLEMEN, THE LINEUPS FOR TODAY'S GAME...

INDULGING IN A LITTLE FANTASY, EH, CHARLIE BROWN? OKAY, LET'S PRETEND I'M THE CATCHER...

ALL RIGHT, PITCHER...WE'VE GOT TO GET OUR SIGNALS STRAIGHT....ONE FINGER WILL MEAN A FAST BALL, TWO FINGERS WILL MEAN A CURVE AND YOU KNOW WHAT THREE FINGERS WILL MEAN?

THREE FINGERS WILL MEAN A SNOWBALL! HA!HA!HA!HA!HA!

HER KIND KNOWS NO SEASON!

SCHULZ

ALL RIGHT! CUT IT OUT!

I ALWAYS THOUGHT MAKING SNOWMEN WAS SUPPOSED TO BE FUN..

SCHULZ

SCHULZ

IF YOU HIT ME WITH THAT SNOWBALL, YOU'RE GONNA BE SORRY!

WOP!

OH, I'M SORRY! YOU'RE RIGHT.. I'M VERY SORRY! I HIT MY OWN SISTER WITH A SNOWBALL, AND NOW I'M REAL SORRY... I'M SO SORRY!

YOU WERE REALLY RIGHT! HOW DID YOU KNOW I'D BE SO SORRY? I'M REALLY SORRY!

POW!

HOW SORRY CAN YOU GET?

SCHULZ

GOOD GRIEF! IT SNOWED LAST NIGHT!

SO HERE I AM COVERED BY A SOFT BLANKET OF SNOW... I THINK I'LL LEAP UP AND SCATTER IT IN ALL DIRECTIONS...

BUT WHAT IF IT **ISN'T** A SOFT BLANKET OF SNOW?

WHAT IF I'M COVERED BY A SHEET OF **ICE**? WHAT IF I'M TRAPPED SO I CAN'T MOVE?

I'VE GOT TO LEAP UP! I'LL COUNT TO THREE AND THEN I'LL LEAP UP... ONE, TWO... WHAT IF IT **IS** ICE? I'LL BE DOOMED! THEY WON'T FIND ME 'TIL NEXT SPRING!

BUT THAT'S NONSENSE! IT MUST BE A SOFT BLANKET OF SNOW! I CAN JUST LEAP UP, AND SCATTER IT IN ALL DIRECTIONS! BUT WHAT IF IT **IS** ICE?!

I'LL BET IT'S ICE! I'LL BET I'M TRAPPED! I'LL BET I'M ALREADY FROZEN TO DEATH! I'LL BET I'M...

HEY, STUPID, WAKE UP! YOU'RE COVERED WITH SNOW!

I'LL NEVER LEARN TO MAKE MY OWN DECISIONS

ARE YOU SURE YOU CAN FIND YOUR WAY HOME NOW?

ABSOLUTELY! WE WON'T HAVE ANY TROUBLE AT ALL

HERE'S THE WORLD WAR I FLYING ACE RECEIVING HIS ORDERS...

SNOOPY HAS A GOOD SENSE OF DIRECTION, DON'T YOU, SNOOPY?

THE RED BARON HAS BEEN SIGHTED OVER CAMBRAI...I MUST BRING HIM DOWN!

I SAID, YOU CAN GET US HOME, CAN'T YOU, SNOOPY?

MY FAITHFUL MECHANICS ARE STANDING BY MY SOPWITH CAMEL...THEY ADMIRE MY CONFIDENT ATTITUDE...

IF YOU DON'T HEAR FROM US, SEND OUT A ST. BERNARD!

AS I WALK ACROSS THE FIELD TO MY PLANE, EVERYONE WAVES....I WAVE BACK.."SO LONG, CHAPS! SO LONG!"

SCHULZ

HELLO?

HELLO, LUCILLE? YOUR KID BROTHER JUST LEFT HERE A FEW MINUTES AGO...MAYBE YOU CAN WATCH FOR HIM SO HE DOESN'T GET LOST... YEAH...HE AND THAT FUNNY LOOKING KID WITH THE BIG NOSE

YEAH, HE TOLD ME THAT WHOLE RIDICULOUS AND IMPOSSIBLE STORY ABOUT THE "GREAT PUMPKIN"....THAT'S THE WILDEST STORY I'VE EVER HEARD...

BUT I BELIEVE IT!!

SCHULZ

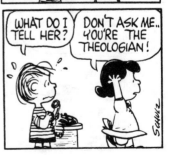

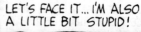

TRICKS OR
TREATS!

BAM!
BAM!
BAM!

WHO WAS IT
THIS TIME, DEAR?

I COULDN'T TELL...
SOME LITTLE KID
IN A DOG COSTUME

CHOMP
CHOMP
CHOMP

NEW YEAR'S DAY AND WHERE AM I? ALONE IN A STRANGE COUNTRY.. WHAT IRONY!

HOW MUCH LONGER CAN THIS WAR GO ON? IF IT DOESN'T END SOON, I THINK I SHALL GO MAD!

GARÇON, ANOTHER ROOT BEER, PLEASE

HOW MANY ROOT BEERS CAN A MAN DRINK? HOW MANY DOES IT TAKE TO DRIVE THE AGONY FROM YOUR BRAIN? CURSE THIS WAR! CURSE THE MUD AND THE RAIN!

AND CURSE YOU TOO, RED BARON, WHEREVER YOU ARE!

I'M GOING TO GET YOU YET! I'M GOING TO SHOOT YOU DOWN

DISTURBANCE? WHO'S CREATING A DISTURBANCE?

I'M A PILOT WITH THE ALLIES! I'M GOING TO SAVE THE WORLD!

YOU CAN'T DO THIS TO A FLYING-ACE! YOU'LL BE SORRY!

GRUMBLE GRUMBLE GRUMBLE GRUMBLE GRUMBLE

SIGH HAPPY NEW YEAR!

SCHULZ

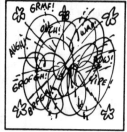

HERE'S THE WORLD WAR I FLYING ACE WALKING ONTO THE FIELD.."GOOD MORNING, CHAPS!" (THESE ARE GOOD LADS)

BUT WHAT'S THIS? THERE'S EXCITEMENT AMONG THE ENLISTED MEN... SOME SORT OF RUMOR GOING ABOUT..

HERE'S THE FLYING ACE REPORTING TO HIS COMMANDING OFFICER... "GOOD MORNING, SIR..A ROOT BEER? YES, SIR, I DON'T MIND IF I DO"

THERE MUST BE SOMETHING BIG COMING UP...HE ONLY OFFERS ME A ROOT BEER WHEN THERE'S A DANGEROUS MISSION TO BE FLOWN!

HERE'S THE WORLD WAR I FLYING ACE TALKING WITH HIS COMMANDING OFFICER...

"ON OUR LEFT IS ST. MIHIEL ...ON OUR RIGHT IS PONT-À-MOUSSON... INTELLIGENCE REPORTS THAT AN AMMUNITION TRAIN IS AT THE RAILWAY STATION IN LONGUYON..."

"OUR BOMBERS CANNOT GET THROUGH, BUT ONE LONE AIRPLANE FLYING VERY LOW JUST MIGHT MAKE IT..."

I, OF COURSE, VOLUNTEER!

JUST BEFORE HE TAKES OFF, THE WORLD WAR I FLYING ACE READS A LETTER FROM HOME..HIS GIRL HAS MARRIED HIS COUSIN WHO WORKS IN A SHIP YARD! WHAT A BITTER BLOW!

BROKEN-HEARTED, THE FLYING ACE CLIMBS INTO HIS SOPWITH CAMEL, AND TAKES OFF TO FLY OVER ENEMY LINES...

SNIF!

SNIF! SNIF!

BUT IT'S NO USE...HE HAS TO TURN AROUND...

SNIF!

HE CAN'T FLY WITH TEARS IN HIS EYES!

YOU CAN'T KEEP THIS UP FOREVER, YOU KNOW..

WHAT ARE YOU GOING TO DO AFTER WORLD WAR I IS OVER?

I HADN'T THOUGHT ABOUT THAT...

MAYBE I'LL DO A LITTLE BARNSTORMING...

HERE'S THE WORLD WAR I FLYING ACE BEING AWAKENED TO FLY ANOTHER DAWN PATROL...

HERE'S THE WORLD WAR I FLYING ACE WALKING OUT ONTO THE FIELD...

IT SNOWED LAST NIGHT... BUT TODAY THE SUN IS OUT..THE SKY IS CLEAR..

I CLIMB INTO THE COCKPIT OF MY SOPWITH CAMEL...

"CHOCKS AWAY"

HERE'S THE WORLD WAR I FLYING ACE ZOOMING THROUGH THE AIR SEARCHING FOR THE RED BARON!

HE DOESN'T HAVE A CHANCE AGAINST MY SUPERIOR WEAPONS, TWO FIXED SYNCHRONISED VICKERS MACHINE GUNS MOUNTED ON TOP OF THE FUSELAGE AND FIRING THROUGH THE AIRSCREW ARC!

POW!

YOU'RE A POOR SPORT, RED BARON

HERE'S THE WORLD WAR I PILOT FLYING OVER ENEMY LINES...

IF I LOSE ANOTHER SOPWITH CAMEL, OUR SUPPLY SERGEANT WILL KILL ME...

OH, NO! IT'S THE RED BARON! HE'S DIVING DOWN OUT OF THE SUN! MACHINE GUN BULLETS RIP THE SIDE OF MY PLANE!

THIS COULD RUIN MY WHOLE DAY..

HERE'S THE WORLD WAR I PILOT DOWN BEHIND ENEMY LINES...

IF I'M CAPTURED, I'LL BE SHOT AT DAWN...

I'LL SNEAK BACK INTO MY DAMAGED SOPWITH CAMEL, AND PUT ON MY SPECIAL DISGUISE..

WO IST DER ROOT BEER HALL?

AH! HE HIT IT RIGHT TO MY SHORTSTOP! THIS'LL BE AN EASY OUT...

HERE'S THE WORLD WAR I FLYING ACE ZOOMING THROUGH THE AIR IN HIS SOPWITH CAMEL..

※ SIGH ※

I THOUGHT I HAD A CLEAN WHITE HANDKERCHIEF IN HERE...

THERE'S A BLUE ONE... A GREEN ONE.. ANOTHER BLUE ONE...

WHAT IN THE WORLD HAPPENED TO MY WHITE HANDKERCHIEF?

THERE IT IS, MEN... FORT ZINDERNEUF!!

HERE'S THE GRIM SOLDIER OF THE FRENCH FOREIGN LEGION STANDING AT HIS POST..

OUR COMPANY IS STATIONED AT FORT ZINDERNEUF ON THE EDGE OF NOWHERE..

AND I? I HAVE A TRAGIC PAST, AND I HAVE JOINED THIS "LEGION OF LOST SOULS" TO FORGET!

I WONDER WHAT IT WOULD BE LIKE TO HAVE A PLAIN OL' "DOG" DOG..

HERE'S "BEAU" SNOOPY OF THE FOREIGN LEGION MARCHING ACROSS THE DESERT

NOTHING BUT SAND AS FAR AS THE EYE CAN SEE...BUZZARDS CIRCLE OVERHEAD...WATER! WE MUST HAVE WATER! WATER...

HERE...YOU LOOKED KIND OF THIRSTY SO I BROUGHT YOU YOUR DISH

WHAT FUN IS THAT?

SCHULZ